Justification
for the

`I0408278`

State

An In-Depth Analysis

By
Will Hammer

"I heartily accept the motto, "That government is best which governs least"; and I should like to see it acted up to more rapidly and systematically. Carried out, it finally amounts to this, which also I believe — "That government is best which governs not at all"; and when men are prepared for it, that will be the kind of government which they will have. Government is at best but an expedient; but most governments are usually, and all governments are sometimes, inexpedient."

— Henry David Thoreau

Contents

Introduction

Part One: Government's Purpose

Part Two: Best Government

Part Three: Social Contract

Part Four: Market Regulation

Part Five: Entitlements

Part Six: National Defense

Part Seven: Protection of Rights

Part Eight: Justice System

Part Nine: Education

Part Ten: Immigration

Part Eleven: Energy

Part Twelve: Jobs

Part Thirteen: Foreign Policy

Part Fourteen: Moral Compass

www.ingramcontent.com/pod-product-compliance
Lightning Source LLC
Chambersburg PA
CBHW071151290526
45788CB00001BA/365